# THIS BOOK BELONGS TO:

_____

THIS BOOK IS DEDICATED TO MY HUSBAND AND ALL THE DREAMERS WHO DREAM OF OPENING A RESTAURANT.

Copyright © 2024 Grow Grit Press LLC. All rights reserved. No part of this book may be reproduced in any form without permission in writing from the publisher. Please send bulk order requests to info@ninjalifehacks.tv

Paperback ISBN: 978-1-63731-927-7
Hardcover ISBN: 978-1-63731-929-1
eBook ISBN: 978-1-63731-928-4

Printed and bound in the USA.
NinjaLifeHacks.tv

Ninja Life Hacks®
by Mary Nhin

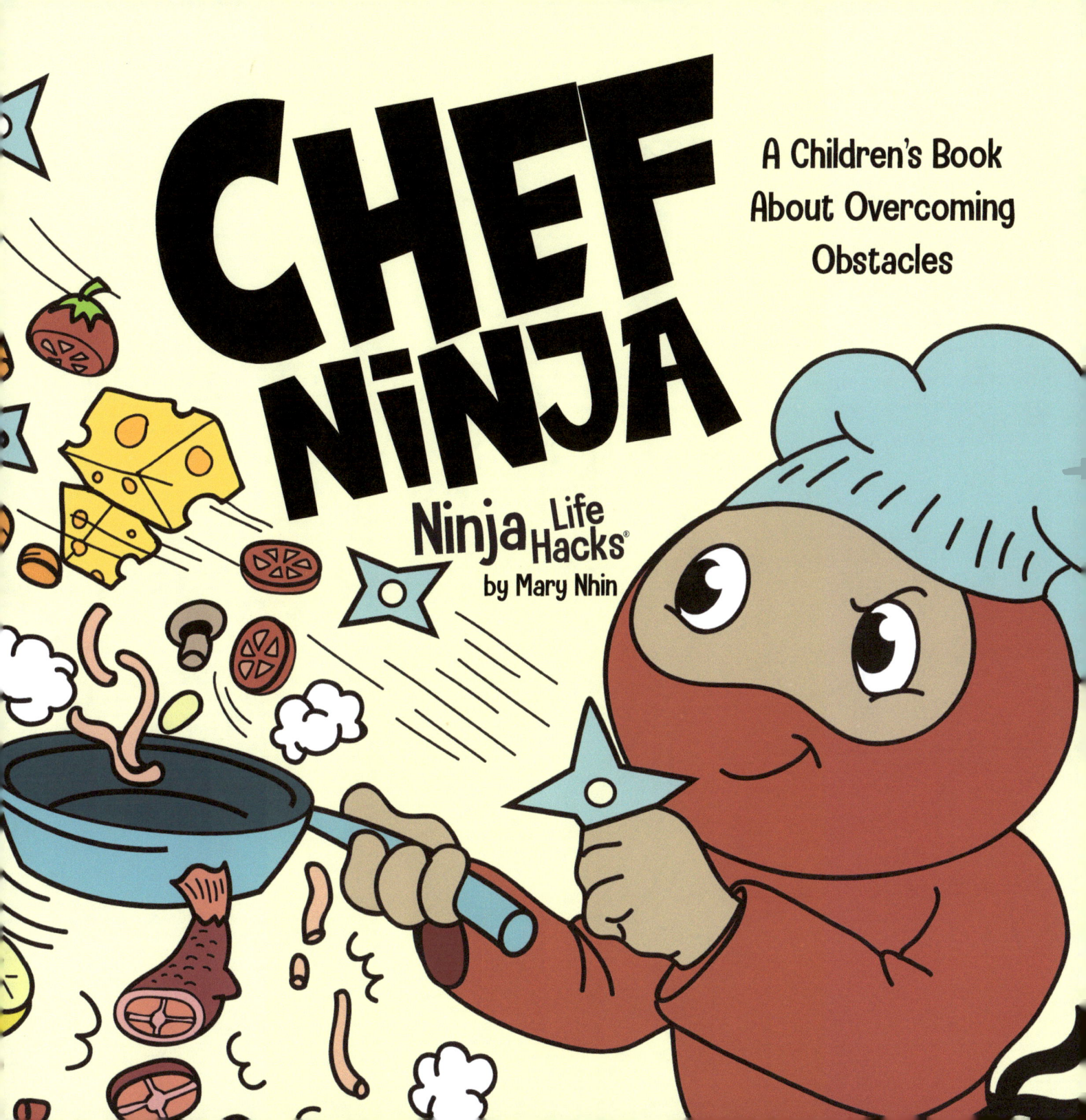

My little place,
It bustled bright,
With joy and cheer
Night after night.

I love to hear from my readers. Email me your feedback or thoughts on what my next story should be at info@ninjalifehacks.tv

Yours truly, Mary

@marynhin  @GrowGrit  #NinjaLifeHacks

Mary Nhin  Ninja Life Hacks

Ninja Life Hacks

@officialninjalifehacks

Continue the learning with fun social, emotional worksheets and printables at ninjalifehacks.tv

Here are two fun, kid-friendly recipes:

## Chef Ninja's Sneaky Sushi Sandwiches

**INGREDIENTS:**
- 4 slices of whole wheat or white bread
- 4 slices of turkey or ham
- 4 slices of cheese (cheddar or your choice)
- 1 cucumber, thinly sliced
- 1 carrot, grated
- 1 avocado, thinly sliced
- Soy sauce for dipping (optional)

**INSTRUCTIONS:**
1. Lay out the slices of bread and use a rolling pin to flatten them slightly.
2. Place a slice of turkey or ham and a slice of cheese on each piece of bread.
3. Add a few slices of cucumber, grated carrot, and avocado on top.
4. Roll up each slice of bread tightly, like a sushi roll.
5. Use a sharp knife to cut the rolls into bite-sized pieces.
6. Arrange the sandwich sushi on a plate and serve with a small bowl of soy sauce for dipping, if desired.

# Ninja Star Veggie Pita Pizzas

### INGREDIENTS:
- Whole wheat pita bread
- 1/2 cup tomato sauce (low sodium)
- 1 cup shredded mozzarella cheese (reduced-fat)
- Assorted veggies (bell peppers, spinach, cherry tomatoes, mushrooms)
- Olive oil spray
- A sprinkle of dried oregano or basil

### INSTRUCTIONS:
1. Preheat your oven to 375°F (190°C) and line a baking sheet with parchment paper.
2. Use a star-shaped cookie cutter to cut the pita bread into star shapes. If you don't have a star cutter, simply use the whole pita as the base.
3. Place the pita stars on the baking sheet and spread a thin layer of tomato sauce on each one.
4. Sprinkle a small amount of shredded mozzarella cheese over the sauce.
5. Top with an assortment of finely chopped veggies. Get creative with your veggie "ninja stars!"
6. Lightly spray the edges of the pita with olive oil and sprinkle with oregano or basil.
7. Bake in the preheated oven for 8-10 minutes, or until the cheese is melted and the edges are slightly crispy.
8. Let them cool a bit, then serve and enjoy your Ninja Star Veggie Pita Pizzas!